A Hike in the Woods

by Betsy Hebert

illustrated by Luanne Marten

"I can't wait for Jeff to get here!" Lee said. Jeff was coming over for the first time and Lee had a great plan for the day.

2

Lee wanted to show Jeff
the **woods** around his house.
The trees were **bare** in winter.
They had lost their leaves.

Lee loved the woods in winter. The **pale** branches were so pretty.

Lee heard a car. "Mom!" he
called. "Jeff is here!"

STOP AND CHECK

What does Lee want
to show Jeff?

The boys ran up to Lee's room.

"What should we do?" asked
Jeff.

Lee said, "I have a surprise."

"What is it?" Jeff asked.

"We're going to hike in the woods," Lee said. "My dad will take us."

Lee pointed out the window. "There is a **creek**. We can hike to it."

Jeff was very quiet.

"I've never been in the woods,"
he said. "It doesn't sound
like fun."

"You should try it!" said Lee.
"I love the woods."

"Okay, I guess I'll go," Jeff said.

STOP AND CHECK

How does Jeff feel about hiking in the woods?

The boys went **outdoors** with Lee's dad. It was cold. But the sun was shining.

"I hope we see deer," said Lee.

The boys looked for animals.
Leaves **crunched** under their
feet.

"Look!" Lee pointed at a rabbit.
Jeff **grinned**.

When they got to the creek, Lee and Jeff sat down. Dad poured hot chocolate. "This is good!" Jeff said.

The boys sat and threw pebbles into the creek. **Drops** of water splashed up.

STOP AND CHECK

What do the boys do at the creek?

Suddenly, a big bird flew out.
Both boys jumped up and saw
the bird **glide** over the water.

"It's just a heron," Dad laughed.

Jeff laughed, too. He said, "You were right, Lee. The woods are great! Now let's find some deer!"

STOP AND CHECK

What makes the boys jump at the creek?

Respond to Reading

Retell

Summarize *A Hike in the Woods.* Use the chart to help you.

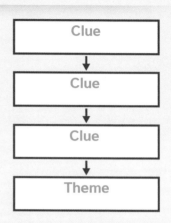

Text Evidence

1. How do Jeff's feelings about the woods change? Theme

2. Read the word *pebbles* on page 12. Use the words and picture. How can you tell what *pebbles* are? Vocabulary

3. Write about the author's message. Write About Reading

Compare Texts

Read a poem about the woods.

The Woods

A bunny bounces by
like a fluffy
rubber ball.

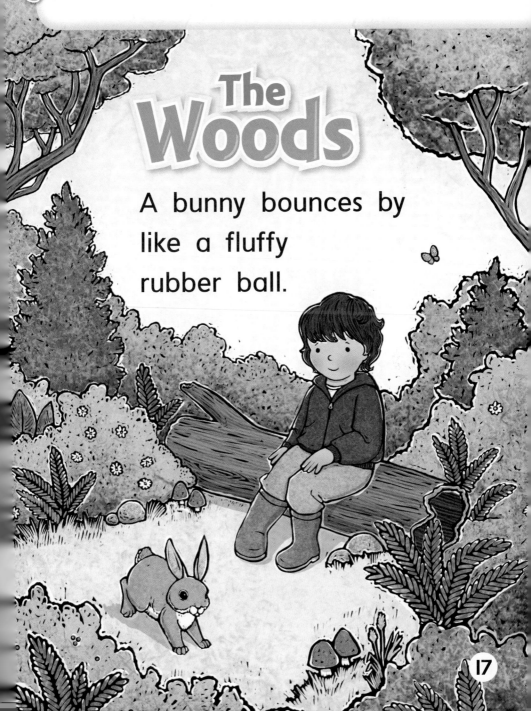

A squirrel scoots
up a tree to
fuss at me.

A fierce fox
barks
from her den.

The woods are wild
and wonderful.

Make Connections

What does the speaker like about the woods? Essential Question

How is the speaker in the poem like Lee? Text to Text

Focus on
Literary Elements

Repetition Repetition means to repeat something. You can repeat a sound, a word, or a phrase.

What to Look for In *The Woods*, sounds are repeated. On page 17 the *b* sound repeats in the words *bunny*, *bounces*, *by*, *rubber*, and *ball*.

Your Turn
What repeats in this part of the poem? *"The woods are wild and wonderful."* Write a sentence with repeating sounds.